For You With Love

For You With Love

How Do I Love Thee?
Let me Count the Ways.

COMPILED BY

SARAH ANNE STUART

BRISTOL PARK BOOKS

The acknowledgements on pages 125 to 126
constitute an extension of the copyright page.

First Bristol Park Books edition published
in 2014

Bristol Park Books
252 W. 38th Street
NYC, NY 10018

Bristol Park Books is a registered trademark
of Bristol Park Books, Inc.

Library of Congress Control Number
2013949095

ISBN:978-0-88486-544-5

Text and cover designed by Cindy LaBreacht

Printed in the United States of America

Contents

Introduction

This collection celebrates the journey of lovers from that very first attraction, through the never-ending commitment of forever and ever. These are poems that have been cherished by generations of lovers and thoughtful expressions by writers who ponder the joys and rewards of loving and being loved.

It is hoped that readers will be inspired to reflect on and enjoy the many pleasures of their own enduring loving relationship.

SARAH ANNE STUART

Attraction

'Tis better to have loved and lost
than never to have loved at all.

ALFRED LORD TENNYSON

I LIKE not only to be loved,
but also to be told I am loved.

GEORGE ELIOT

What Care I

Shall I, wasting in despair,
Die because a woman's fair?
Or my cheeks make pale with care
'Cause another's rosy are?

Be she fairer than the day
Or the flowery meads in May—
　　If she be not so to me,
　　What care I how fair she be?

Great or good, or kind or fair,
I will ne'er the more despair;
If she love me, this believe,
I will die ere she shall grieve;

If she slight me when I woo,
I can scorn and let her go.
　　For if she be not for me,
　　What care I for whom she be?

GEORGE WITHER

IF YOU would be loved,
love and be loveable.

BENJAMIN FRANKLIN

Jenny Kissed Me

Jenny kissed me when we met,
Jumping from the chair she sat in.
Time, you thief, who love to get
Sweets into your list, put that in.
Say I'm weary, say I'm sad;
Say that health and wealth have missed me;
Say I'm growing old, but add—
Jenny kissed me!

LEIGH HUNT

FIRST LOVE is only a little foolishness
and a lot of curiosity.

GEORGE BERNARD SHAW

We Parted in Silence

We parted in silence, we parted by night,
On the banks of that lonely river;
Where the fragrant limes their boughs unite,
We met—and we parted forever!
The night-bird sung, and the stars above
Told many a touching story,
Of friends long passed to the kingdom of love,
Where the soul wears its mantle of glory.

And now on the midnight sky I look,
And my heart grows full of weeping;
Each star is to me a sealed book,
Some tale of that loved one keeping.
We parted in silence,—we parted in tears,
On the banks of that lovely river:
But the odor and bloom of those bygone years
Shall hang o'er its waters forever.

MRS. CRAWFORD

IMAGINATION is at the root of much
that passes for love.

GILBERT PARKER

No Time to Hate

I had no time to hate, because
The grave would hinder me,
And life was not so ample I
Could finish enmity.

Nor had I time to love, but since
Some industry must be,
The little toil of love, I thought,
Was large enough for me.

EMILY DICKINSON

FRIENDSHIP is certainly the finest balm
for the pangs of disappointed love.

JANE AUSTEN

April Love

We have walked in Love's land a little way,
　　We have learnt his lesson a little while,
And shall we not part at the end of day,
　　With a sigh, a smile?

A little while in the shine of the sun,
　　We were twined together, joined lips, forgot
How the shadows fall when the day is done,
　　And when Love is not.

We have made no vows—there will none be broke,
　　Our love was free as the wind on the hill,
There was no word said we need wish unspoke,
　　We have wrought no ill.

So shall we not part at the end of day,
　　Who have loved and lingered a little while,
Join lips for the last time, go our way,
　　With a sigh, a smile?

ERNEST DOWSON

Summer Days

In summer, when the days were long,
We walked together in the wood:
Our heart was light, our step was strong;
Sweet flutterings were there in our blood,
In summer, when the days were long.

We strayed from morn till evening came;
We gathered flowers, and wove us crowns;
We walked mid poppies red as flame,
Or sat upon the yellow downs;
And always wished our life the same.

In summer, when the days were long,
We leaped the hedgerow, crossed the brook;
And still her voice flowed forth in song,
Or else she read some graceful book,
In summer, when the days were long.

We loved, and yet we knew it not,—
For loving seemed like breathing then;
We found a heaven in every spot;
Saw angels, too, in all good men;
And dreamed of God in grove and grot.

In summer, when the days were long,
Alone I wander, muse alone.
I see her not; but that old song
Under the fragrant wind is blown,
In summer, when the days are long.

Alone I wander in the wood:
But one fair spirit hears my sighs;
And half I see, so glad and good,
The honest daylight of her eyes,
That charmed me under earlier skies.

In summer, when the days are long,
I love her as we loved of old.
My heart is light, my step is strong;
For love brings back those hours of gold,
In summer, when the days are long.

AUTHOR UNKNOWN

A PAIR of powerful spectacles has sometimes
sufficed to cure a person of love.

FREIDRICH NIETZSCHE

THE MAGIC of first love is our ignorance
that it can ever end.

BENJAMIN DISRAELI

Just Then

The other day
You looked at me.
You did not say,
"I love you,"
But just then you believed it.

LOIS WYSE

LOVE IS a smoke made
with the fume of sighs.

WILLIAM SHAKESPEARE

The First Time

The first time that the sun rose on thine oath
To love me, I looked forward to the moon
To slacken all those bonds which seemed too soon
And quickly tied to make a lasting troth.
Quick-loving hearts, I thought, may quickly loathe;
And, looking on myself, I seemed not one
For such man's love!—more like an out of tune
Worn viol, a good singer would be wroth
To spoil his song with, and which, snatched in haste
Is laid down at the first ill-sounding note.
I did not wrong myself so, but I placed
A wrong on *thee*. For perfect strains may float
Neath master-hands, from instruments defaced,—
And great souls, at one stroke, may do and doat.

ELIZABETH BARRETT BROWNING

Miss You

Miss you, miss you, miss you;
    Everything I do
Echoes with the laughter
    And the voice of You.

You're on every corner,
    Every turn and twist,
Every old familiar spot
    Whispers how you're missed.

Miss you, miss you, miss you!
    Everywhere I go
There are poignant memories
    Dancing in a row.

Silhouette and shadow
    Of your form and face,
Substance and reality
    Everywhere displace.

Oh, I miss you, miss you!
    God! I miss you, Girl!
There's a strange, sad silence
    'Mid the busy whirl,

Just as tho' the ordinary
    Daily things I do
Wait with me, expectant
    For a word from You.

Miss you, miss you, miss you!
    Nothing now seems true
Only that 'twas heaven
    Just to be with You.

DAVID CORY

Why, Lovely Charmer!
FROM "THE HIVE"

Why, lovely charmer, tell me why,
So very kind, and yet so shy?
Why does that cold, forbidding air
Give damps of sorrow and despair?
Or why that smile my soul subdue,
And kindle up my flames anew?

In vain you strive with all your art,
By turns to fire and freeze my heart;
When I behold a face so fair,
So sweet a look, so soft an air,
My ravished soul is charmed all o'er,
I cannot love thee less or more.

AUTHOR UNKNOWN

VANITY is as ill at ease under indifference as tenderness is under a love which it cannot return.

GEORGE ELIOT

Sly Thoughts

"I saw him kiss your cheek!"—
" 'T is true."
"O Modesty!"—" 'T was strictly kept:
He thought me asleep; at least, I knew
He thought I thought he thought I slept."

COVENTRY PATMORE

THE HUNGER for love is much more difficult to remove than the hunger for bread.

MOTHER TERESA

She was a Phantom of Delight

She was a phantom of delight
When first she gleamed upon my sight;
A lovely apparition, sent
To be a moment's ornament;
Her eyes as stars of twilight fair;
Like Twilight's, too, her dusky hair;
But all things else about her drawn
From May-time and the cheerful dawn;
A dancing shape, an image gay,
To haunt, to startle, and waylay.

I saw her upon nearer view,
A spirit, yet a woman too!
Her household motions light and free,
And steps of virgin-liberty;
A countenance in which did meet
Sweet records, promises as sweet;
A creature not too bright or good
For human nature's daily food,
For transient sorrows, simple wiles,
Praise, blame, love, kisses, tears, and smiles.

And now I see with eye serene
The very pulse of the machine;
A being breathing thoughtful breath,
A traveller between life and death:

The reason firm, the temperate will,
Endurance, foresight, strength, and skill;
A perfect woman, nobly planned
To warn, to comfort, and command;
And yet a spirit still, and bright
With something of an angel-light.

WILLIAM WORDSWORTH

At the Church Gate

Although I enter not,
Yet round about the spot
Ofttimes I hover;
And near the sacred gate,
With longing eyes I wait,
Expectant of her.

The minister bell tolls out
Above the city's rout,
And noise and humming;
They've hushed the minister bell;
The organ 'gins to swell;
She's coming, coming!

My lady comes at last,
Timid and stepping fast,
And hastening hither,
With modest eyes downcast;
She comes,—she's here, she's past!
May Heaven go with her!

Kneel undisturbed, fair saint!
Pour out your praise or plaint
Meekly and duly;
I will not enter there,

To sully your pure prayer
With thoughts unruly.

But suffer me to pace
Round the forbidden place,
Lingering a minute,
Like outcast spirits, who wait,
And see, through heaven's gate,
Angels within it.

WILLIAM MAKEPEACE THACKERAY

Shall I Compare Thee to a Summer's Day?

Shall I compare thee to a summer's day?
Thou art more lovely and more temperate:
Rough winds do shake the darling buds of May,
And summer's lease hath all too short a date;
Sometime too hot the eye of heaven shines,
And often is his gold complexion dimm'd;
And every fair from fair sometime declines,
By chance or nature's changing course untrimm'd:
But thy eternal summer shall not fade
Nor lose possession of that fair thou ow'st;
Nor shall Death brag thou wand'rest in his shade,
When in eternal lines to time thou grow'est;
So long as men can breathe or eyes can see,
So long lives this, and this gives life to thee.

WILLIAM SHAKESPEARE

Longing

Come to me in my dreams, and then
By day I shall be well again!
For then the night will more than pay
The hopeless longing of the day.

Come, as though cam'st a thousand times,
A messenger from radiant climes,
And smile on thy new world, and be
As kind to others as to me!

Or, as thou never cam'st in sooth,
Come now, and let me dream it truth;
And part my hair, and kiss my brow,
And say: *My love! why sufferest thou?*

Come to me in my dreams, and then
By day I shall be well again!
For then the night will more than pay
The hopeless longing of the day.

MATTHEW ARNOLD

A Love Song

By the fierce flames of Love I'm in a sad taking,
I'm singed like a pig that is hung up for bacon,
My stomach is scorched like an over-done mutton-chop,
That for want of gravy wont afford a single drop.
Love, love, love is like a dizziness,
Wont let a poor man go about his business.

My great toes and little toes are burnt to a cinder,
As a hot burning-glass burns a dish-cloth to tinder,
As cheese by a hot salamander is roasted,
By beauty that's red-hot, like a cheese am I toasted.
Love, love, love is like a dizziness,
Wont let a poor man go about his business.

Attend all young lovers, who after ladies dandle,
I'm singed like a duck's foot over a candle,
By this that and t'other I'm treated uncivil,
Like a gizzard I'm peppered, and then made a devil.
Love, love, love is like a dizziness,
Wont let a poor man go about his business.

ROYALL TYLER

ABSENCE diminishes mediocre passions and increases great ones, as the wind extinguishes candles and fans fires.

FRANCOISE DE LA ROCHEFOUCAULD

Delight in Disorder

A sweet disorder in the dress
Kindles in clothes a wantonness:
A lawn about the shoulders thrown
Into a fine distraction,
An erring lace, which here and there
Enthralls the crimson stomacher,
A cuff neglectful, and thereby
Ribbands to flow confusedly,
A winning wave (deserving note)
In the tempestuous petticoat,
A careless shoe-string, in whose tie
I see a wild civility,
Do more bewitch me, than when art
Is too precise in every part.

ROBERT HERRICK

When We Two Parted

When we two parted
In silence and tears,
Half broken-hearted
    To sever for years,
Pale grew thy cheek and cold,
    Colder thy kiss;
Truly that hour foretold
    Sorrow to this.

In secret we met—
    In silence I grieve
That thy heart could forget,
    Thy spirit deceive.
If I should meet thee
    After long years,
How should I greet thee?—
    With silence and tears.

GEORGE GORDON, LORD BYRON

The Light of Love

Each shining light above us
Has its own peculiar grace;
But every light of heaven
Is in my darling's face.

For it is like the sunlight,
So strong and pure and warm,
That folds all good and happy things,
And guards from gloom and harm.

And it is like the moonlight,
So holy and so calm;
The rapt peace of a summer night,
When soft winds die in balm.

And it is like the starlight;
For, love her as I may,
She dwells still lofty and serene
In mystery far away.

JOHN HAY

If It Be True that
Any Beauteous Thing

If it be true that any beauteous thing
Raises the pure and just desire of man
From earth to God, the eternal fount of all,
Such I believe my love; for as in her
So fair, in whom I all besides forget,
I view the gentle work of her Creator,
I have no care for any other thing,
Whilst thus I love. Nor is it marvellous,
Since the effect is not of my own power,
If the soul doth, by nature tempted forth,
Enamored through the eyes,
Repose upon the eyes which it resembleth,
And through them riseth to the Primal Love,
As to its end, and honors in admiring;
For who adores the Maker needs must love his work.

MICHAELANGELO
Translation of J.E. Taylor

A Woman's Question

Before I trust my fate to thee,
Or place my hand in thine,
Before I let thy future give
Color and form to mine,
Before I peril all for thee,
Question thy soul to-night for me.

I break all slighter bonds, nor feel
A shadow of regret:
Is there one link within the past
That holds thy spirit yet?
Or is thy faith as clear and free
As that which I can pledge to thee?

Does there within thy dimmest dreams
A possible future shine,
Wherein thy life could henceforth breathe
Untouched, unshared by mine?
If so, at any pain or cost,
O, tell me before all is lost!

Is there within thy heart a need
That mine cannot fulfil?
One chord that any other hand
Could better wake or still?
Speak now, lest at some future day
My whole life wither and decay.

Couldst thou withdraw thy hand one day
And answer to my claim,
That fate, and that to-day's mistake,—
Not thou,—had been to blame?
Some soothe their conscience thus; but thou
Wilt surely warn and save me now.

Nay, answer *not*,—I dare not hear,
The words would come too late;
Yet I would spare thee all remorse,
So comfort thee, my fate:
Whatever on my heart may fall,
Remember, I *would* risk it all!

ADELAIDE ANNE PROCTER

Surrender

There is no remedy for love
but to love more.

HENRY DAVID THOREAU

A LOVING heart is the beginning
of all knowledge.

THOMAS CARLYLE

How Do I Love Thee?
Let Me Count the Ways

How do I love thee? Let me count the ways.
I love thee to the depth and breadth and height
My soul can reach, when feeling out of sight
For the ends of Being and ideal Grace.
I love thee to the level of every day's
Most quiet need; by sun and candle-light.
I love thee freely, as men strive for Right;
I love thee purely, as they turn from Praise.
I love thee with the passion put to use
In my old griefs, and with my childhood's faith.
I love thee with a love I seemed to lose
With my lost saints,—I love thee with the breath,
Smiles, tears, of all my life!—and, if God choose,
I shall but love thee better after death.

ELIZABETH BARRETT BROWNING

Earth Trembles Waiting

I wait for his foot fall,
Eager, afraid,
Each evening hour
When the lights fade...

I wait for his voice
To speak low to me—
As a mariner lost
Dreams of harbor, at sea...

I wait for his lips
When the dusk falls.
Life holds my longing
Behind dark walls.

I wait for his face—
As after rain
Earth trembles waiting
For the sun again...

BLANCHE SHOEMAKER WAGSTAFF

A Red, Red, Rose

O my Luve's like a red, red rose,
That's newly sprung in June:
O my Luve's like the melodie
That's sweetly played in tune!

As fair art thou, my bonnie lass,
So deep in luve am I;
And I will luve thee still, my dear,
Till a' the seas gang dry.

Till a' the seas gang dry, my dear,
And the rocks melt wi' the sun;
I will luve thee still, my dear,
While the sands o' life shall run.

And fare thee weel, my only Luve,
And fare thee weel a while!
And I will come again, my Luve,
Though it were ten thousand mile.

ROBERT BURNS

A Birthday

My heart is like a singing bird
    Whose nest is in a watered shoot:
My heart is like an apple tree
    Whose boughs are bent with thickset fruit;
My heart is like a rainbow shell
    That paddles in a halcyon sea;
My heart is gladder than all these
    Because my love is come to me.

Raise me a dais of silk and down;
    Hang it with vair and purple dyes;
Carve it in doves and pomegranates,
    And peacocks with a hundred eyes;
Work it in gold and silver grapes,
    In leaves and silver fleurs-de-lys;
Because the birthday of my life
    Is come, my love is come to me.

CHRISTINA ROSSETTI

AT THE TOUCH of love
everyone becomes a poet.

PLATO

Understanding

I do not know the words
Of that small song in my heart,
But somehow, my dear,
I think you do.

LOIS WYSE

"I LOVE YOU, love you, love you!" she said.
"If you were to cast me off now—but you will not—
you would never be rid of me."

CHARLES DICKENS

A Message

If there is any way, dear Lord
In which my heart may send her word
Of my continued love,
And of my joy in her relief
From pain—a joy not even grief
And loneliness may rise above,

Reveal it to me... for I long
To keep intact the tie so strong
Between us, from my birth,
That when we meet (as meet we must)
There shall be naught but perfect trust,
Such as we always knew on earth!

ANNA NELSON REED

Believe Me, if all Those Endearing Young Charms

Believe me, if all those endearing young charms,
    Which I gaze on so fondly today,
Were to change by tomorrow, and fleet in my arms,
    Like fairy-gifts fading away,
Thou wouldst still be adored, as this moment thou art,
    Let thy loveliness fade as it will,
And around the dear ruin each wish of my heart
    Would entwine itself verdantly still.

It is not while beauty and youth are thine own,
    And thy cheeks unprofaned by a tear,
That the fervour and faith of a soul can be known,
    To which time will but make thee more dear;
No, the heart that has truly loved never forgets,
    But as truly loves on to the close,
As the sunflower turns on her god, when he sets,
    The same look which she turned when he rose.

THOMAS MOORE

The White Flag

I sent my love two roses,—one
As white as driven snow,
And one a blushing royal red,
A flaming Jacqueminot.

I meant to touch and test my fate;
That night I should divine,
The moment I should see my love,
If her true heart were mine.

For if she holds me dear, I said,
She'll wear my blushing rose;
If not, she'll wear my cold Lamarque,
As white as winter's snows.

My heart sank when I met her: sure
I had been overbold,
For on her breast my pale rose lay
In virgin whiteness cold.

Yet with low words she greeted me,
With smiles divinely tender;
Upon her cheek the red rose dawned,—
The white rose meant surrender.

JOHN HAY

A VERY small degree of hope is sufficient
to cause the birth of love.

STENDAHL

At Nightfall

I need so much the quiet of your love
    After the day's loud strife;
I need your calm all other things above
    After the stress of life.

I crave the haven that in your dear heart lies,
    After all toil is done;
I need the starshine of your heavenly eyes,
    After the day's great sun.

CHARLES HANSON TOWNE

LOVE IS of all passions the strongest,
for it attacks simultaneously the head,
the heart, and the senses.

LAO TZU

Forgiven

You left me when the weary weight of sorrow
  Lay, like a stone, upon my bursting heart;
It seemed as if no shimmering tomorrow
  Could dry the tears that you had caused to start.
You left me, never telling why you wandered—
  Without a word, without a last caress;
Left me with but the love that I had squandered,
  The husks of love and a vast loneliness.

And yet if you came back with arms stretched toward me,
  Came back tonight, with carefree, smiling eyes,
And said: "My journeying has somehow bored me,
  And love, though broken, never, never dies!"
I would forget the wounded heart you gave me,
  I would forget the bruises on my soul.
My old-time gods would rise again to save me;
  My dreams would grow supremely new and whole.

What though youth lay, a tattered garment, o'er you?
  Warm words would leap upon my lips, long dumb;
If you came back, with arms stretched out before you,
  And told me, dear, that you were glad to come!

MARGARET E. SANGSTER

She Walks in Beauty

She walks in beauty, like the night
Of cloudless climes and starry skies,
And all that's best of dark and bright
Meet in her aspect and her eyes;
Thus mellowed to that tender light
Which heaven to gaudy day denies.

One shade the more, one ray the less,
Had half impaired the nameless grace
Which waves in every raven tress
Or softly lightens o'er her face,
Where thoughts serenely sweet express
How pure, how dear their dwelling-place.

And on that check and o'er that brow
So soft, so calm, yet eloquent,
The smiles that win, the tints that glow
But tell of days in goodness spent,
A mind at peace with all below,
A heart whose love is innocent.

GEORGE GORDON, LORD BYRON

To Celia

Drink to me only with thine eyes,
    And I will pledge with mine;
Or leave a kiss but in the cup
    And I'll not look for wine.
The thirst that from the soul doth rise
    Doth ask a drink divine;
But might I of Jove's nectar sup,
    I would not change for thine.

I sent thee late a rosy wreath,
    Not so much honoring thee
As giving it a hope that there
    It could not withered be;
But thou thereon didst only breathe
    And sent'st it back to me;
Since when it grows, and smells, I swear,
    Not of itself but thee!

BEN JONSON

WHO, being loved, is poor?

OSCAR WILDE

The Bargain

My true love hath my heart, and I have his,
    By just exchange one for another given:
I hold his dear, and mine he cannot miss,
    There never was a better bargain driven:
       My true love hath my heart, and I have his.

His heart in me keeps him and me in one,
    My heart in him his thoughts and senses guides:
He loves my heart, for once it was his own,
    I cherish his because in me it bides:
       My true love hath my heart, and I have his.

SIR PHILIP SIDNEY

LOVE, though said to be afflicted with blindness,
is a vigilant watchman.

CHARLES DICKENS

To Her Absent Sailor

FROM "THE TENT ON THE BEACH"

Her window opens to the bay,
On glistening light or misty gray,
And there at dawn and set of day
In prayer she kneels:
"Dear Lord!" she saith, "to many a home
From wind and wave the wanderers come;
I only see the tossing foam
Of stranger keels.

"Blown out and in by summer gales,
The stately ships, with crowded sails,
And sailors leaning o'er their rails,
Before me glide;
They come, they go, but nevermore,
Spice-laden from the Indian shore,
I see his swift-winged Isidore
The waves divide.

"O dread and cruel deep, reveal
The secret which thy waves conceal,
And, ye wild sea-birds, hither wheel
And tell your tale.

Let winds that tossed his raven hair
A message from my lost one bear,—
Some thought of me, a last fond prayer
Or dying wail!

"Come, with your dreariest truth shut out
The fears that haunt me round about;
O God! I cannot bear this doubt
That stifles breath.
The worst is better than the dread;
Give me but leave to mourn my dead
Asleep in trust and hope, instead
Of life in death!"

It might have been the evening breeze
That whispered in the garden trees,
It might have been the sound of seas
That rose and fell;
But, with her heart, if not her ear,
The old loved voice she seemed to hear:
"I wait to meet thee: be of cheer
For all is well!"

JOHN GREENLEAF WHITTIER

A Wish

Mine be a cot beside the hill;
A bee-hive's hum shall soothe my ear;
A willowy brook that turns a mill,
With many a fall shall linger near.

The swallow, oft, beneath my thatch
Shall twitter from her clay-built nest;
Oft shall the pilgrim lift the latch,
And share my meal, a welcome guest.

Around my ivied porch shall spring
Each fragrant flower that drinks the dew;
And Lucy, at her wheel, shall sing
In russet gown and apron blue.

The village-church among the trees,
Where first our marriage-vows were given,
With merry peals shall swell the breeze
And point with taper spire to heaven.

SAMUEL ROGERS

Love is Not All:
It is Not Meat Nor Drink

Love is not all: it is not meat nor drink
Nor slumber nor a roof against the rain;
Nor yet a floating spar to men that sink
And rise and sink and rise and sink again;
Love cannot fill the thickened lung with breath,
Nor clean the blood, nor set the fractured bone;
Yet many a man is making friends with death
Even as I speak, for lack of love alone.
It well may be that in a difficult hour,
Pinned down by pain and moaning for release,
Or nagged by want past resolution's power,
I might be driven to sell your love for peace,
Or trade the memory of this night for food.
It well may be. I do not think I would.

EDNA ST. VINCENT MILLAY

Come, Rest in This Bosom

FROM "IRISH MELODIES"

Come, rest in this bosom, my own stricken deer,
Though the herd have fled from thee, thy home is still here;
Here still is the smile, that no cloud o'ercast,
And a heart and a hand all thy own to the last.

Oh! what was love made for, if 'tis not the same
Through joy and through torment, through glory and shame?
I know not, I ask not, if guilt's in that heart,
I but know that I love thee, whatever thou art.

Thou hast called me thy Angel in the moments of bliss,
And thy Angel I'll be, mid the horrors of this,
Through the furnace, unshrinking, thy steps to pursue,
And shield thee, and save thee,—or perish there too!

THOMAS MOORE

Destiny

Somewhere there waiteth in this world of ours
For one lone soul another lonely soul—
Each chasing each through all the weary hours,
And meeting strangely at one sudden goal;
Then blend they—like green leaves with golden flowers,
Into one beautiful and perfect whole—
And life's long night is ended, and the way
Lies open onward to eternal day.

EDWIN ARNOLD

IS LOVE a tender thing?
It is too rough, too rude, too boisterous;
and it pricks like thorns.

WILLIAM SHAKESPEARE

Song

Shall I love you like the wind, love,
That is so fierce and strong,
That sweeps all barriers from its path
And recks not right or wrong?
The passion of the wind, love,
Can never last for long.

Shall I love you like the fire, love,
With furious heat and noise,
To waken in you all love's fears
And little of love's joys?
The passion of the fire, love,
Whate'er it finds; destroys.

I will love you like the stars, love,
Set in the heavenly blue,
That only shine the brighter
After weeping tears of dew;
Above the wind and fire, love,
They love the ages through!

And when this life is o'er, love,
With all its joys and jars,
We'll leave behind the wind and fire
To wage their boisterous wars,—
Then we shall only be, love,
The nearer to the stars!

R.W. RAYMOND

If Thou Must Love Me

If thou must love me, let it be for naught
Except for love's sake only. Do not say
"I love her for her smile…her look…her way
Of speaking gently,—for a trick of thought
That falls in well with mine, and certes brought
A sense of pleasant ease on such a day."
For these things in themselves, beloved, may
Be changed, or change for thee,—and love so wrought,
May be unwrought so. Neither love me for
Thine own dear pity's wiping my cheeks dry,—
A creature might forget to weep, who bore
Thy comfort long, and lose thy love thereby.
But love me for love's sake, that evermore
Thou mayst love on, through love's eternity.

ELIZABETH BARRETT BROWNING

I Love You

I love your lips when they're wet with wine
    And red with a wild desire;
I love your eyes when the lovelight lies
    Lit with a passionate fire.
I love your arms when the strands enmesh
    Your kisses against my face.

Not for me the cold, calm kiss
    Of a virgin's bloodless love;
Not for me the saint's white bliss,
    Nor the heart of a spotless dove.
But give me the love that so freely gives
    And laughs at the whole world's blame,
With your body so young and war in my arms,
    It set my poor heart aflame.

So kiss me sweet with your warm wet mouth,
    Still fragrant with ruby wine,
And say with a fervor born of the South
    That your body and soul are mine.
Clasp me close in your warm young arms,
    While the pale stars shine above,
And we'll live our whole young lives away
    In the joys of a living love.

ELLA WHEELER WILCOX

Commitment

Love is composed of a single soul
inhabiting two bodies.

ARISTOTLE

ALL mankind loves a lover.

RALPH WALDO EMERSON

Love Not Me for Comely Grace

Love not me for comely grace,
    For my pleasing eyes or face,
Not for any outward part,
No, nor for a constant heart:
    For these may fail or turn to ill,
        So thou and I shall sever:

Keep, therefore, a true woman's eye,
And love me still but know not why—
    So hast thou the same reason still
        To dote upon me ever!

AUTHOR UNKNOWN

My True Love Hath My Heart

My true love hath my heart, and I have his,
By just exchange, one for the other given.
I hold his dear, and mine he cannot miss,
There never was a better bargain driven.
His heart in me keeps me and him in one,
My heart in him his thoughts and senses guides;
He loves my heart, for once it was his own,
I cherish his, because in me it bides.
His heart his wound received from my sight;
My heart was wounded with his wounded heart;
For as from me on him his hurt did light,
So still methought in me his hurt did smart.
Both equal hurt, in this change sought our bliss:
My true love hath my heart and I have his.

SIR PHILIP SIDNEY

Sometimes Imperfect, Often Impossible

You are
Sometimes imperfect,
Often impossible

And I still love you

Because, my sweet, you are
The only man in the world
Who makes me feel
At home in the world

Even though I am
Sometimes imperfect,
Often impossible

LOIS WYSE

A Bridge Instead of a Wall

They say a wife and husband, bit by bit,
    Can rear between their lives a mighty wall,
So thick they can not talk with ease through it,
    Nor can they see across, it stands so tall!
Its nearness frightens them but each alone
    Is powerless to tear its bulk away,
And each, dejected, wishes he had known
    For such a wall, some magic thing to say.

So let us build with master art, my dear,
    A bridge of faith between your life and mine,
A bridge of tenderness and very near
    A bridge of understanding, strong and fine—
        Till we have formed so many lovely ties
        There never will be room for walls to rise!

AUTHOR UNKNOWN

LOVE many things, for therein lies true strength,
and whoever loves much performs much,
and can accomplish much, and what is done
in love is done well.

VINCENT VAN GOGH

The Human Touch

"Tis the human touch in this world that counts,
The touch of your hand and mine,
Which means far more to the fainting heart
Than shelter and bread and wine;
For shelter is gone when the night is o'er,
And bread lasts only a day,
But the touch of the hand and the sound of the voice
Sing on in the soul alway.

SPENCER MICHAEL FREE

IF YOU press me to say why I loved him, I can say
no more than because he was he, and I was I.

MICHEL DE MONTAIGNE

The Newlyweds

"What is the thing your eyes hold loveliest
In these, our fields and shores? I'll bring it home."
With tenderness, awaiting her request,
He stood. The dooryard dogwood was a foam
Of wind-tipped flowers, catching at her breath,
But these she did not mention, trying hard
To meet his eagerness. "Come flood, or death
By thunderbolt," he laughed, "I'll heap the yard
With everything you ask for. Name it now."
She made no answer, yet a little smile
Marked for him her compliance. Then, the bough
Tilted its stiffened beauty like a pile
Of snowy cloud above them. "Ah, I know,"
He cried, "Your heart is set on something far
Beyond our present means. Is that not so?"
"I want you and the dogwood as you are,
April forever. Can you heap that here?"
And while she watched, the boy went out of him.
"I think I understand your wifely fear,"
And, reaching up, he shook a weighted limb.
So, like the blossoms, quiet settled there.
"I will not run away to bring you gifts."

He spoke less lightly. "Boys can never bear
The undramatic thing. Their rich blood lifts
Their spirits higher than their hands, but men
May learn where such as you will teach,
How life is spent at try and try again
To keep white-blowing loveliness in reach."

CLOYD MANN CRISWELL

Because You Love Me

Because you love me, I have found
New joys that were not mine before;
New stars have lightened up my sky
With glories growing more and more.
Because you love me I can rise
To the heights of fame and realms of power;
Because you love me I may learn
The highest use of every hour.

Because you love me I can choose
To look through your dear eyes and see
Beyond the beauty of the Now
Far onward to Eternity.

Because you love me I can wait
With perfect patience well possessed;
Because you love me all my life
Is circled with unquestioned rest;
Yes, even Life and even Death
Is all unquestioned and all blest.

PALL MALL MAGAZINE

I Think I Love You

Once, when we were very young,
You looked at me and said,
"I think I love you."
And I bristled slightly
(as young girls do).
And I said to you, "Think?
You only think you love me?
You mean you do not know?"

For at that moment I knew love.
I was on intimate terms with Cole Porter lyrics,
and I cried when I read *Wuthering Heights*.

But now that I have grown up
I know the timeless treasure of your words.
For love must have a way to grow,
And you found the way so long ago.
You took the time to think our love...
And still you do.
A good love takes thinking through.
And living with.
And I knew
The first morning I awoke and touched you next to me...
I, too, could say,
"I think I love you."

LOIS WYSE

Upon the Sand

All love that has not friendship for its base,
Is like a mansion built upon the sand.
Though brave its walls as any in the land,
And its tall turrets lift their heads in grace;
Though skillful and accomplished artists trace
Most beautiful designs on every hand,
And gleaming statues in dim niches stand,
And fountains play in some flow'r-hidden place:

Yet, when from the frowning east a sudden gust
Of adverse fate is blown, or sad rains fall
Day in, day out, against its yielding wall,
Lo! the fair structure crumbles to the dust.
Love, to endure life's sorrow and earth's woe,
Needs friendship's solid masonwork below.

ELLA WHEELER WILCOX

AS SOON go kindle a fire with snow, as seek to quench
the fire of love with words.

WILLIAM SHAKESPEARE

A Gift

See! I give myself to you, Beloved!
My words are little jars
For you to take and put upon a shelf.
Their shapes are quaint and beautiful,
And they have many pleasant colors and lustres
To recommend them.
Also the scent from them fills the room
With sweetness of flowers and crushed grasses.

When I shall have given you the last one
You will have the whole of me,
But I shall be dead.

AMY LOWELL

TIME is too slow for those who wait, too swift
for those who fear, too long for those who grieve,
too short for those who rejoice, but for those
who love, time is eternity.

HENRY VAN DYKE

Marriage
FROM "HUMAN LIFE"

Then before All they stand,—the holy vow
And ring of gold, no fond illusions now,
Bind her as his. Across the threshold led,
And every tear kissed off as soon as shed,
His house she enters,—there to be a light,
Shining within, when all without is night;
A guardian o'er his life presiding,
Doubling his pleasures and his cares dividing,
Winning him back when mingling in the throng,
Back from a world we love, alas! too long,
To fireside happiness, to hours of ease,
Blest with that charm, the certainty to please.
How oft her eyes read his; her gentle mind
To all his wishes, all his thoughts inclined;
Still subject,—ever on the watch to borrow
Mirth of his mirth and sorrow of his sorrow!
The soul of music slumbers in the shell,
Till waked and kindled by the master's spell,
And feeling hearts—touch them but rightly—pour
A thousand melodies unheard before!

SAMUEL ROGERS

LOVE is a great beautifier.

LOUISA MAY ALCOTT

The Night Has a Thousand Eyes

The night has a thousand eyes,
    And the day but one;
Yet the light of the bright world dies
    With the dying sun.

The mind has a thousand eyes,
    And the heart but one;
Yet the light of a whole life dies
    When love is done.

FRANCIS WILLIAM BOURDILLON

LOVE. It is said, is blind; but love is not blind.
It is an extra eye, which shows us what is most
worthy of regard. To see the best is to see most
clearly, and that is the lover's privilege.

JAMES M. BARRIE

Let Me Not to the Marriage of True Minds

Let me not to the marriage of true minds
Admit impediments. Love is not love
Which alters when it alteration finds,
Or bends with the remover to remove:
O, no! it is an ever-fixed mark,
That looks on tempests and is never shaken;
It is the star to every wandering bark,
Whose worth's unknown, although his height be taken.
Love's not Time's fool, though rosy lips and cheeks
Within his bending sickle's compass come;
Love alters not with his brief hours and weeks,
But bears it out even to the edge of doom.
    If this be error, and upon me prov'd,
    I never writ, nor no man ever lov'd.

WILLIAM SHAKESPEARE

One Day I Wrote Her Name Upon the Strand

One day I wrote her name upon the strand;
But came the waves, and washed it away:
Again, I wrote it with a second hand;
But came the tide, and made my pains his prey.
Vain man, said she, that dost in vain assay
A mortal thing so to immortalize;
For I myself shall like to this decay,
And eke my name be wiped out likewise.
Not so, quoth I; let baser things devise
To die in dust, but you shall live by fame:
My verse your virtues rare shall eternize,
And in the heavens write your glorious name.
Where, whenas death shall all the world subdue,
Our love shall live, and later life renew.

EDMUND SPENSER

Love Is of God

Beloved, let us love: love is of God;
In God alone hath love its true abode.

Beloved, let us love: for they who love,
They only, and His sons, born from above.

Beloved, let us love: for love is rest,
And he who loveth not abides unblest.

Beloved, let us love: for love is light,
And he who loveth not dwelleth in night.

Beloved, let us love: for only thus
Shall we behold that God Who loveth us.

HORATIUS BONAR

Absence

What shall I do with all the days and hours
That must be counted ere I see thy face?
How shall I charm the interval that lowers
Between this time and that sweet time of grace?

Shall I in slumber steep each weary sense,—
Weary with longing? Shall I flee away
Into past days, and with some fond pretence
Cheat myself to forget the present day?

Shall love for thee lay on my soul the sin
Of casting from me God's great gift of time?
Shall I, these mists of memory locked within,
Leave and forget life's purposes sublime?

O, how or by what means may I contrive
To bring the hour that brings thee back more near?
How may I teach my drooping hope to live
Until that blessed time, and thou art here?

I'll tell thee; for thy sake I will lay hold
Of all good aims, and consecrate to thee,
In worthy deeds, each moment that is told
While thou, beloved one! art for from me.

For thee I will arouse my thoughts to try
All heavenward flights, all high and holy strains;
For thy dear sake I will walk patiently
Through these long hours, nor call their minutes pains.

I will this dreary blank of absence make
A noble task-time; and will therein strive
To follow excellence, and to o'ertake
More good than I have won since yet I live.

So may this doomed time build up in me
A thousand graces, which shall thus be thine;
So may my love and longing hallowed be,
And thy dear thought an influence divine.

FRANCES ANNE KEMBLE

I Love You

I love you
Not for what
I want you to be
But for what you are

I loved you then
For what you were
I love you now
For what you have become

I miss you
And not only you

I miss what I am
When you are here...

LEONARD NIMOY

Because

Because you come to me with naught save love,
And hold my hand and lift mine eyes above,
A wider world of hope and joy I see,
Because you come to me.

Because you speak to me in accents sweet,
I find the roses walking round my feet,
And I am led through tears of joy to see,
Because you speak to me.

Because God made thee mine I'll cherish thee
Through light and darkness, through all time to be,
And pray His love may make our lives divine.
Because God made thee mine.

EDWARD TESCHEMACHER

And I Have You

Rain has drops   Sun has shine
Moon has beams   That make you mine

Rivers have banks   Sands for shores
Hearts have heartbeats   That make me yours

Needles have eyes   Though pins may prick
Elmer has glue   To make things stick

Winter has Spring   Stockings feet
Pepper has mint   To make it sweet

Teachers have lessons   Soup du jour
Lawyers sue bad folks   Doctors cure

All and all this much is true
You have me   And I have you

NIKKI GIOVANNI

Living Together

Faith makes all things possible . . .
love makes all things easy.

DWIGHT L. MOODY

A Poem of Friendship

We are not lovers
because of the love
we make
but the love we have

We are not friends
because of the laughs
we share
but the tears
we save

I don't want to be near you
for the thoughts we share
but the words we never have
to speak

I will never miss you
because of what we do
but what we are
together

NIKKI GIOVANNI

Together

You and I by this lamp with these
Few books shut out the world. Our knees
Touch almost in this little space.
But I am glad. I see your face.
The silences are long, but each
Hears the other without speech.
And in this simple scene there is
The essence of all subtleties,
The freedom from all fret and smart,
The one sure Sabbath of the heart.

The world—we cannot conquer it,
Nor change the minds of fools one whit.
Here, here alone do we create
Beauty and peace inviolate;
Here night by night and hour by hour
We build a high impregnable tower
Whence may shine, now and again,
A light to light the feet of men
When they see the rays thereof:
And this is marriage, this is love.

LUDWIG LEWISOHN

Sweet is the Sunbreak

Sweet is
    The sunbreak
    After the rain

Welcome is
    The breeze
    That follows the heat

Warm is
    The fire
    Against the snow

Yet none
    So precious
    As your smile
That says

      Welcome home...

    After we've
      Been apart

LEONARD NIMOY

Love

I love you,
Not only for what you are,
But for what I am
When I am with you.

I love you,
Not only for what
You have made of yourself,
But for what
You are making of me.

I love you
For the part of me
That you bring out;
I love you
For putting your hand
Into my heaped-up heart
And passing over
All the foolish, weak things
That you can't help
Dimly seeing there,
And for drawing out
Into the light
All the beautiful belongings
That no one else had looked
Quite far enough to find.

I love you because you
Are helping me to make
Of the lumber of my life
Not a tavern
But a temple;
Out of the works
Of my every day
Not a reproach
But a song...

AUTHOR UNKNOWN

THE GREATEST happiness of life
is the conviction that we are loved;
loved for ourselves, or rather,
loved in spite of ourselves.

VICTOR HUGO

Prayer of any Husband

Lord, may there be no moment in her life
When she regrets that she became my wife,
And keep her dear eyes just a trifle blind
To my defects, and to my failings kind!

Help me to do the utmost that I can
To prove myself her measure of a man,
But, if I often fail as mortals may,
Grant that she never sees my feet of clay!
And let her make allowance—now and then—
That we are only grown-up boys, we men,
So, loving all our children, she will see,
Sometimes, a remnant of the child in me!

Since years must bring to all their load of care,
Let us together every burden bear,
And when Death beckons one its path along,
May not the two of us be parted long!

MAZIE V. CARUTHERS

Tell Her So

Amid the cares of married strife
    In spite of toil and business life
If you value your dear wife—
    Tell her so!

When days are dark and deeply blue
    She has her troubles, same as you
Show her that your love is true
    Tell her so!

Whether you mean or care,
Gentleness, kindness, love, and hate,
Envy, anger, are there.
Then, would you quarrels avoid
And peace and love rejoice?
Keep anger not only out of your words—
Keep it out of your voice.

AUTHOR UNKNOWN

Not Ours the Vows

Not ours the vows of such as plight
Their troth in sunny weather,
While leaves are green, and skies are bright
To walk on flowers together.

But we have loved as those who tread
The thorny path of sorrow,
With clouds above, and cause to dread
Yet deeper gloom tomorrow.

That thorny path, those stormy skies,
Have drawn our spirits nearer;
And rendered us, by sorrow's ties,
Each to the other dearer.

AUTHOR UNKNOWN

A WOMAN knows the face of the man she loves,
as a sailor knows the open sea.

HONORE DE BALZAC

Do You Need Me?

Remember that day in New York?
You know, the last day we were there.
I had just bought the pink suit
(the one with the funny loops you like so much).
I walked out of the store,
And I saw one of those there-on-the-sidewalk phone booths
So I called the hotel for messages.
The operator read all the usual nothings.
And then she came to that message from you.
It said, "Do you need me? I'll be at…"
Funny.
I never heard where you'd be.
I heard only
"Do you need me?"
And I thought,
"Do I need you?"
And slowly I put the receiver back on the hook
And I said to myself…
Oh, how I need you.
This very moment I need you.
How dear you are. How right that you should show me what
"I love you"
Really means.

LOIS WYSE

Need of Loving

Folk need a lot of loving in the morning;
  The day is all before, with cares beset—
The cares we know, and they that give no warning;
  For love is God's own antidote for fret.

Folk need a heap of loving at the noontime—
  In the battle lull, the moment snatched from strife—
Halfway between the waking and the croon time,
  While bickering and worriment are rife.

Folk hunger so for loving at the nighttime,
  When wearily they take them home to rest—
At slumber song and turning-out-the-light time—
  Of all the times for loving, that's the best.

Folk want a lot of loving every minute—
  The sympathy of others and their smile!
Till life's end, from the moment they begin it,
  Folks need a lot of loving all the while.

STRICKLAND GILLIAN

from *Rabbi Ben Ezra*

Grow old along with me!
The best is yet to be,
The last of life, for which the first was made:
Our times are in his hand
Who saith: "A whole I planned,
Youth shows but half; trust God, see all, nor be afraid."

Ah, but a man's reach should exceed his grasp,
Or what's a heaven for?

ROBERT BROWNING

LOVE is a flower that grows in any soil, works
its sweet miracles undaunted by autumn frost
or winter snow, blooming fair and fragrant all
the year, and blessing those who give and those
who receive.

LOUISA MAY ALCOTT

To My Friend

I have never been rich before,
But you have poured
Into my heart's high door
A golden hoard.

My wealth is the vision shared,
The sympathy,
The feast of the soul prepared
By you for me.

Together we wander through
The wooded ways.
Old beauties are green and new
Seen through your gaze.

I look for no greater prize
Than your soft voice.
The steadiness of your eyes
Is my heart's choice.

I have never been rich before,
But I divine
Your step on my sunlit floor
And wealth is mine!

ANNE CAMPBELL

A Private Place

There is within each of us
A private place
For thinking private thoughts
And dreaming private dreams.

But in the shared experience of marriage,
Some people cannot stand the private partner.

How fortunate for me
That you have let me grow,
Think my private thoughts,
Dream my private dreams.

And bring a private me
To the shared experience of marriage.

LOIS WYSE

BEING deeply loved by someone gives you
strength, while loving someone deeply gives
you courage.

LAO TZU

The Wife to Her Husband

Linger not long. Home is not home without thee:
Its dearest tokens do but make me mourn.
O, let its memory, like a chain about thee,
Gently compel and hasten thy return!

Linger not long. Though crowds should woo thy staying,
Bethink thee, can the mirth of thy friends, though dear,
Compensate for the grief thy long delaying
Costs the fond heart that sighs to have thee here?

Linger not long. How shall I watch thy coming,
As evening shadows stretch o'er moor and dell;
When the wild bee hath ceased her busy humming,
And silence hangs on all things like a spell!

How shall I watch for thee, when fears grow stronger,
As night grows dark and darker on the hill!
How shall I weep, when I can watch no longer!
Ah! art thou absent, art thou absent still?

Yet I should grieve not, though the eye that seeth me
Gazeth through tears that make its splendor dull;
For oh! I sometimes fear when thou art with me,
My cup of happiness is all too full.

Haste, haste thee home to thy mountain dwelling,
Haste, as a bird unto its peaceful nest!
Haste, as a skiff, through tempests wide and swelling,
Flies to its haven of securest rest!

AUTHOR UNKNOWN

Sonnet

My Love, I have no fear that thou shouldst die;
Albeit I ask no fairer life than this,
Whose numbering-clock is still thy gentle kiss,
While Time and Peace with hands unlocked fly,—
Yet care I not where in Eternity
We live and love, well knowing that there is
No backward step for those who feel the bliss
Of Faith as their most lofty yearnings high:
Love hath so purified my being's core,
Meseems I scarcely should be startled, even,
To find, some morn, that thou hadst gone before;
Since, with thy love, this knowledge too was given,
Which each calm day doth strengthen more and more,
That they who love are but one step from Heaven.

JAMES RUSSELL LOWELL

THERE is no religion without love, and people
may talk as much as they like about their religion,
but if it does not teach them to be good and kind
to man and beast it is all a sham.

ANNA SEWELL

The Poet's Song to His Wife

How many summers, love,
Have I been thine?
How many days, thou dove,
Hast thou been mine?
Time, like the winged wind
When 't bends the flowers,
Hath left no mark behind,
To count the hours!

Some weight of the thought, though loath,
On thee he leaves;
Some lines of care round both
Perhaps he weaves;
Some fears,—a soft regret
For joys scarce known;
Sweet looks we half forget;—
All else is flown!

Ah!—With what thankless heart
I mourn and sing!
Look, where our children start,
Like sudden spring!
With tongues all sweet and low
Like a pleasant rhyme,
They tell how much I owe
To thee and time!

BARRY CORNWALL

Marriage

I know we loved each other when we walked
So long ago in spring beneath the moon;
When, hand clasped close in hand, we softly talked
Of that new joy our hearts would shelter soon,
Perennially golden and secure
From any change. But O, we could not see
That springtime wonderment would not endure
As first it was but alter blessedly.
We could not know, my dear, we could not guess
How years augment the miracles of love;
How autumn brings a depth of tenderness
That is beyond young April's dreaming of!
How there would burn a richer flame some day
Than that which first threw glory on our way.

A. WARREN

Midcentury Love Letter

Stay near me. Speak my name. Oh, do not wander
By a thought's span, heart's impulse, from the light
We kindle here. You are my sole defender
(As I am yours) in this precipitous night,
Which over earth, till common landmarks alter,
Is falling, without stars, and bitter cold.
We two have but our burning selves for shelter.
Huddle against me. Give me your hand to hold.

So might two climbers lost in mountain weather
On a high slope and taken by the storm,
Desperate in the darkness, cling together
Under one cloak and breathe each other warm.
Stay near me. Spirit, perishable as bone,
In no such winter can survive alone.

PHYLLIS McGINLEY

Silhouette

Here is the house
Where the roof swings low,
And the lilacs against
The afterglow;

The friendly shadows
Of elm and yew,
And a ragged space
Where a star peeps through;

And clear and dear,
Where the firelight lures,
A form in the doorway
I know is yours!

ETHEL JACOBSON

LOVE is a better teacher than duty.

ALBERT EINSTEIN

KEEP love in your heart. A life without it is like a sunless garden when the flowers are dead.

OSCAR WILDE

True Love

True love is but a humble, low-born thing,
And hath its food served up in earthenware;
It is a thing to walk with, hand in hand,
Through the everdayness of this work-day world,
Baring its tender feet to every roughness,
Yet letting not one heart-beat go astray
From beauty's law of plainness and content—
A simple, fireside thing, whose quiet smile
Can warm earth's poorest hovel to a home.

JAMES RUSSELL LOWELL

The 5:32

She said, if tomorrow my world were torn in two,
Blacked out, dissolved, I think I would remember
(As if transfixed in surrendering amber)
This hour best of all the hours I knew:
When cars came backing into the shabby station,
Children scuffing the seats, and the women driving
With ribbons around their hair, and the trains arriving,
And the men getting off with tired but practiced motion.

Yes, I would remember my life like this, she said:
Autumn, the platform red with Virginia creeper,
And a man coming toward me, smiling, the evening paper
Under his arm, and his hat pushed back on his head;
And wood smoke lying like haze on the quiet town,
And dinner waiting, and the sun not yet gone down.

PHYLLIS McGINLEY

LOVE begins at home, and it is not
how much we do, but how much love
we put in that action.

MOTHER TERESA

A Cozy Heart

Once I though that love
Was tempestuous,
Tumultuous,
"Kiss me quick."

I was wrong.

Love is usually a very comfortable way of life,
A cozy heart,
Kisses on the cheek,
"Wear your rubbers and blow your nose."

And what keeps a love so cozy?
The fact that every so often love is
Tempestuous, tumultuous...
"Kiss me quick."

LOIS WYSE

To My Dear and Loving Husband

If ever two were one, then surely we.
If ever man were loved by wife, then thee;
If ever wife was happy in a man,
Compare with me ye women if you can.
I prize thy love more than whole mines of gold,
Or all the riches that the East doth hold.
My love is such that rivers cannot quench,
Nor ought but love from thee give recompense.
Thy love is such I can no way repay;
The heavens reward thee manifold, I pray.
Then while we live, in love let's so persever,
That when we live no more we may live ever.

ANNE BRADSTREET

Forever and Ever

Love is the only thing that
we can carry with us when we go,
and it makes the end so easy.

LOUISA MAY ALCOTT

WE LOVE LIFE, not because we are used to living but because we are used to loving.

FRIEDRICHE NIETZSCHE

House and Home

A house is built of logs and stone,
Of tiles and posts and piers;
A home is built of loving deeds
That stand a thousand years.

VICTOR HUGO

ONCE the realization is accepted that even between the closest human beings infinite distances continue, a wonderful living side-by-side can grow; they can succeed in loving the distance between them, which makes it possible for each to see the other whole against the sky.

RAINER MARIA RILKE

Old Letters

I keep your letters for a rainy day;
Then take them out and read them all again.
So, reading, I forget that skies are gray,
And pathways sodden under falling rain.

They are so full of simple friendliness,—
Of understanding of the things I love.
No phrase obscure or vague, to make me guess,—
No deep philosophy my soul to move.

And though your eyes are "lifted to the hills"
You still keep faith with earth, and earthy things;
Prosaic duty all your hour fills
The while you listen for the beat of wings.

You have read deeply in the book of life,
And you have added lines that I shall keep
To be a shield against the petty strife
Until such time as I shall fall asleep.

So when I would forget that skies are gray
I read your letters on a rainy day.

ADELE JORDAN TARR

A Good Love Works
Because A Good Love Works

There really is no pattern
To a love that works.
Do her neuroses
Fit his psychoses?
Does his spaghetti
Match her sauce?
Don't ask me, my dear.

All I know for sure
Is that our love still works
So long as you can tell me
We are going to have two whole days together
. . . and I am glad.

LOIS WYSE

WE LOVED with a love that was more than love.

EDGAR ALLAN POE

The Unquiet Grave

"The wind doth blow today, my love,
And a few small drops of rain;
I never had but one true love,
In cold grave she was lain.

"I'll do as much for my true love
As any young man may;
I'll sit and mourn all at her grave
For a twelvemonth, and a day."

"The twelvemonth and a day being up,
The dead began to speak,
"Oh who sits weeping on my grave,
And will not let me sleep?"

"'Tis I, my love, sits on your grave
And will not let you sleep,
For I crave one kiss of your clay-cold lips
And that is all I seek."

"You crave one kiss of clay-cold lips,
But my breath smells earthy strong;
If you have one kiss of my clay-cold lips
Your time will not be long:

"'Tis down in yonder garden green,
Love, where we used to walk,

The finest flower that ere was seen
Is withered to a stalk.

"The stalk is withered dry, my love,
So will our hearts decay;
So make yourself content, my love,
Till God calls you away."

AUTHOR UNKNOWN

O, Lay Thy Hand in Mine, Dear!

O, lay thy hand in mine, dear!
We're growing old;
But Time hath brought no sign, dear,
That hearts grow cold.
'T is long, long since our new love
Made life divine;
But age enricheth true love,
Like noble wine.

O, lean thy life on mine, dear!
'T will shelter thee.
Thou wert a winsome vine, dear,
On my young tree:
And so, till boughs are leafless,
And songbirds flown,
We'll twine, then lay us, griefless,
Together down.

GERALD MASSEY

THE WAY to love anything
is to realize that it may be lost.

GILBERT K CHESTERTON

Time

    Time is
Too slow for those who Wait,
Too swift for those who Fear,
Too long for those who Grieve,
Too short for those who Rejoice;
But for those who Love
    Time is
    Eternity.

AUTHOR UNKNOWN

LOVE is the beauty of the soul.

SAINT AUGUSTINE

A Little While I Fain Would Linger Yet

A little while (my life is almost set!)
I fain would pause along the downward way,
Musing an hour in this sad sunset ray,
While, Sweet! our eyes with tender tears are wet:
A little hour I fain would linger yet.

A little while I fain would linger yet,
All for love's sake, for love that cannot tire;
Though fervid youth be dead, with youth's desire,
And hope had faded to a vague regret,
A little while I fain would linger yet.

A little while I fain would linger here:
Behold! who knows what strange, mysterious bars
'Twixt souls that love may rise in other stars?
Nor can love deem the face of death is fair:
A little while I still would linger here.

A little while, when light and twilight meet,—
Behind, our broken years; before, the deep
Weird wonder of the last unfathomed sleep,—
A little while I still would clasp thee, Sweet,
A little while, when night and twilight meet.

A little while I fain would linger here;
Behold! who knows what soul-dividing bars
Earth's faithful loves may part in other stars?
Nor can love deem the face of death is fair:
A little while I still would linger here.

PAUL HAMILTON HAYNE

A Farewell

With all my will, but much against my heart,
We two now part.
My Very Dear,
Our solace is, the sad road lies so clear.
It needs no art,
With faint, averted feet
And many a tear,
In our opposed paths to persevere.
Go thou to East, I West.
We will not say
There's any hope, it is so far away.
But, O my Best,
When the one darling of our widowhead,
The nursing Grief,
Is dead,
And no dews blur our eyes
To see the peach-bloom come in evening skies,
Perchance we may,
Where now this night is day,
And even through faith of still averted feet,
Making full circle of our banishment,
Amazed meet;
The bitter journey to the bourne so sweet
Seasoning the termless feast of our content
With tears of recognition never dry.

COVENTRY PATMORE

When She Must Go

When she must go, so much will go with her!
Stories of country summers, far and bright,
Wisdom of berries, flowers and chestnut bur,
And songs to comfort babies in the night;

Old legends and their meanings, half-lost tunes,
Wise craftsmanship in all the household ways,
And roses taught to flower in summer noons,
And children taught the shaping of good days;

A heart still steadfast, stable, that can know
A son's first loss, a daughter's first heartbreak,
And say to them, "This, too, shall pass and go;
This is not all!" while anguished for their sake;

Courage to cling to when the day is lost,
Love to come back to when all love grows cold,
Quiet from tumult; heart fire from the frost.
Oh, must she ever go, and we be old?

MARGARET WIDDEMER

LOVE all, trust a few,
do wrong to none.

WILLIAM SHAKESPEARE

Let's Do It All Over Again

Let's do it
　　All over again
　　Starting from
　　　　The beginning

Let us re-touch
　　Every step
　　Along the way

All the joys, fears
　　Laughter and tears
　　That brought us as
　　　　Close
　　As we are
　　　　Today
　　Let's do it all

　　　　All over again

LEONARD NIMOY

Should You Go First

Should you go first and I remain
To walk the road alone,
I'll live in memory's garden, dear,
With happy days we've known.

In Spring I'll wait for roses red,
When fades the lilac blue,
In early fall, when brown leaves call
I'll catch a glimpse of you.

Should you go first and I remain
For battles to be fought,
Each thing you've touched along the way
Will be a hallowed spot.
I'll hear your voice, I'll see your smile,
Though blindly I may grope,
The memory of your helping hand
Will buoy me on with hope.

Should you go first and I remain
To finish with the scroll,
No length'ning shadows shall creep in
To make this life seem droll.
We've known so much of happiness,
We've had our cup of joy,

And memory is one gift of God
That death cannot destroy.

Should you go first and I remain,
One thing I'd have you do:
Walk slowly down that long, lone path,
For soon I'll follow you.
I'll want to know each step you take
That I may walk the same,
For some day down that lonely road
You'll hear me call your name.

A.K. ROWSWELL

LET US always meet each other
with a smile, for the smile
is the beginning of love.

MOTHER TERESA

Heart-To-Heart

There is a cord
Unseen
That binds us heart-to-heart,
The surest way
For me to shorten the cord
Is to let you choose the length.

For if I choose to tighten
That unseen cord
By poking,
Prying,
Wondering,
Why?-ing,
You will dissolve the cord
And create
An unseen wall
For both of us to see.

And that, my beloved,
Would be the tragedy
Of this
Or any
Marriage.

LOIS WYSE

And I Am Old to Know

No place seemed farther than your death
but when I went there—gone from there,
it was from your love you spoke
and it was to your love I moved.

And as you speak it—you, my own:
in the days, in the nights of your voice,
always the word of love opens,
opens into all its meaning.

And as I longer move to you,
as you wait and as you take me,
not like a lover but like love
you tell me and I am old to know:

love is to the farthest place—
love is to so far a place
from always its greatest distances,
to see where death was, I look back.

PAULINE HANSON

A LOVING HEART is the truest wisdom.

CHARLES DICKENS

Acknowledgments

Nikki Giovanni. "A Poem of Friendship" from
Cotton Candy On a Rainy Day. Copyright © 1978
by Nikki Giovanni. "I Have You" from *Love Poems*.
Copyright © 1997 by Nikki Giovanni.
Reprinted with the permission of the author.

Phyllis McGinley "the5:32" copyright © 1960
by Phyllis McGinley, copyright renewed © 1988
by Patricia Hayden Blake. Reprinted with
the permission of Curtis Brown Ltd.
"Midcentury Love Letter" copyright © 1954
by Phyllis McGinley, copyright renewed © 1982
by Phyllis Hayden Blake. First appeared in
The Love Letters of Phyllis McGinley published
by The Viking Press . Reprinted with the permission
of Curtis Brown Ltd.

Leonard Nimoy "I Love You," "Let's Do It All Over
Again" and "Sweet is the Sunbreak" from *A Lifetime
of Love*. Copyright © 2002 by Leonard Nimoy.
Reprinted with the permission of Rumbleseat
Productions, Inc.

Contributors